All rights reserved. No part of this publication may be reproduced, distributed, or transmitted in any form or by any means, including photocopying, recording, or other electronic or mechanical methods, without the prior written permission of the publisher, except in the case of brief quotations embodied in critical reviews and certain other noncommercial uses permitted by copyright law. For permission requests, write to the publisher, with the subject line: "Permission Request: The Transfer Publishing," at the e-mail address below.

Cover Illustration Copyright © 2014 by Adrion Butler
www.adrionbutler.wix.com
Author photograph by Swamp Graphics
Bible references used within the Fair Use Guidelines as described in the Zondervan NKJV bible published Copyright © 2007 by Zondervan.

The Transfer Publishing
djonesministries@gmail.com
djonesministries.com

© 2014 The Transfer Publishing

AT THE POINT OF ELEVATION

DAMION JONES

FORWARD

There are many leaders in the world today, however, there are few leaders that will shape the very core of their generation. Damion Jones is a revolutionary leader that God has called specifically in this generation to shift the mindset of the culture. In a time when many people are in search of identity in an ever changing world. Damion Jones gives a very open a transparent articulation of the process into self-discovery. This is more than just a book of information it is a testimony of how a person can make it through various phases of life and come out on the other side victorious. When reading the pages of this book you see the power of God's Grace. Damion tells his personal story and how he went through ups and downs, his struggles, and his triumphs. After you read this book it will activate in you dreams, purpose, and destiny that have been lying dormant. You will be motivated and encouraged to go after everything that God called you to. I encourage you to read every page with an open mind and allow the Spirit of the Lord to speak to you. I believe that this book is a prophetic declaration to this generation of seekers that there is hope. This book is right on time and in time. I would like to say to my friend Pastor Damion Jones job well done on this work of literature. I am honored to know you and call you friend. This book is a major deposit in the Earth by an anointed and willing vessel of the Kingdom of God. This book is guaranteed to push you to your "Point of Elevation."

Pastor Torrey Montgomery

Lead Pastor
Connection Church

CEO/Founder
Greater Kingdom Works International

"This literary work is a perfect mixture of intellect and passion. Housed within these pages are answers for the spirit and life to the soul."

- Dr. Johnasen L. Pack
Visionary of The Jordan Partnership
Senior Pastor of Bridge Builders International Church

ACKNOWLEDGMENTS

I would like to thank God through my Lord and savior Jesus Christ. I would like to thank my wife for her unwavering commitment and support in the process of producing this book. Thank you mom for the encouragement during tough times. I would like to thank my children for their patience and understanding during this process. I would like to thank the Generational Transfer Church family for the love and support that was given during this project. Last but not least, my mentor and spiritual father for all of your encouragement, direction and covering during this process. My prayer is that this book will prepare those that are looking for answers and direction for their point of elevation.

-Pastor Damion Jones

TABLE OF CONTENTS

I. IN THE BEGINNING (pg. 1)

II. BUILDING CONFIDENCE (pg.13)

III. YOU CAN BE THE BEST TOO (pg. 25)

IV. YOUR RELATIONSHIPS: DO THEY HELP OR HINDER? (pg. 30)

V. DESTINY KILLERS (pg. 37)

VI. TIRED (pg. 44)

VII. TESTING GROUND (pg. 51)

VIII. TRANSITION (pg. 58)

IX. PASSION (pg. 64)

X. AT THE POINT OF ELEVATION (pg. 70)

Chapter 1

IN THE BEGINNING

Zechariah 4:10 NLT, "*Do not despise these small beginnings, for the LORD rejoices to see the work begin, to see the plumb line in Zerubbabel's hand.*"

In the beginning years of your life you may have felt as if things were not set in your favor for you to be successful. You may have been told you were not the most handsome, athletic, courageous, or most intelligent branch on the tree.

I lived the first ten years of my life in a single parent, low income home environment. There was no money set aside for college, no inheritance or any signs of anything to look forward to. So as beginnings go, it appeared as if my chances of being successful were slim to none.

Such circumstances can sometimes dictate the direction you will steer your life. The beginning is not an end all be all for your life because most of these things are subject to

IN THE BEGINNING

change. It is only the inception of your development as a person, athlete, educator or whatever God has purposed you to do.

You may not believe you are an attractive young man or woman, but after God gets through developing you, you may cultivate the features needed to be the show stopper or entrance maker.

In the introduction to his book, <u>Journey to Significance</u>[1], Tony Miller helps me to put this in perspective...he says, "Find the explorer spirit buried deep within you, one who would love to participate in God's plan...no matter what! This implies that we will have to dig to get to heart of who we are in God and that it is not a surface treasure.

How many family members or friends can you think of who showed you their childhood photos which are in stark contrast to how they look or appear today? Have you ever gone on the World Wide Web and seen pictures of your favorite celebrity of how they started out in the early years of their careers and how you are shocked at the transformation that occurred as time went on?

Your current state does not dictate where you will end up according to **Job 8:7a The Message**, *"Even though you're not much right* *now, you'll end up better than ever."*

I believe that God uses life situations and encounters to develop us into the marvelous, elevated masterpieces that we are to become.

For example, there are forces at work above and below the planet's surface. From the water's edge to the tallest peaks, physical forces work through time to shape the landforms of the planet.[2] In like manner, God allows forces both natural and spiritual to infiltrate our lives in order to get us to the level of elevation He planned before the Earth was framed.

Yes, in some cases, you are a reflection of what you have been through, nonetheless, your experiences make you stronger. They also enhance your knowledge and cultivate certain wisdoms needed in life. Appreciate the beginning and learn all that you can learn whether it be in relationships, the workplace or in family situations.

In the beginning, as well as in the future days on this journey we call life, never stop learning. There is nothing too insignificant that you can't learn from it whether you're at the level of a child or senior citizen.

When we first begin a process or work toward a goal, we have a tendency to seek

IN THE BEGINNING

validation through what we see others do. Remember that God made you unique. There is something great that you bring to the table that completes the picture of His overall plan. That is why God tells us in **Ephesians 1:4 NKJV**, *"just as He chose us in*
Him before the foundation of the world, that we should be holy and without blame before Him in love,".

Our experiences prepare us for that point of elevation. We are all different. Only God knows what makes us tick. He knows what it's going to take to bring out the very best in you. The Bible says his thoughts are not like our thoughts. (See **Isaiah 55:9**) and that He takes the foolish things to confound the wise. (See **1 Corinthians 1:27**)

IF AT FIRST...

I recall a conversation with a young man who was extremely frustrated with the results he received in the early stages of his business endeavors. He explained how he was tired of getting the same result. As I looked into his situation I could see how he was letting his beginning experience kill his drive to persevere and try again.

The first set of results does not necessarily determine whether your plan or idea will work. Chalk them up to a learning experience. You've probably heard the old adage…"*If at first you don't succeed, try and try again!*" ~ **W. E. Hickson**

Draw as much knowledge and wisdom out of those challenges as you can. Make it profitable for you. Just because it didn't work the first, second or even the third time, doesn't mean the task is impossible to accomplish.

There was a time in my youth when I thought that because I wasn't as athletic, tall, or as strong as my cousins that I would always be last in everything. I honestly believed that because I didn't have the traits or abilities that they possessed that I was inadequate. I believed I had gotten the short end of the stick.

I had to come to the realization that there is something great in me too. I had to grasp that I was a work in progress and this was only the beginning. Sometimes our perception of ourselves can hinder the potential that is inside of us. Would you agree? Especially, if our personal perception is inaccurate.

I know people who think that they are ugly, but they could probably be models if they wanted to. I know people who think they are fat or overweight but there are people who would love to be their size. Some of them are the appropriate weight for their height. A false perception will ultimately drive you to abort your dreams.

It is my prayer that if this is you, that you will develop the right perception which is obtained through reading your Bible to find out what God says about you and your future and then believing and accepting it's truths.

Truths such as **Jeremiah 29:11NKJV,** *"For I know the thoughts that I think toward you, says the Lord, thoughts of peace and not of evil, to give you a future and a hope."* And **Psalm 139:14 NKJV,** *"I will praise You, for I am fearfully and wonderfully made; Marvelous are Your works, And that my soul knows very well.*

EVERYONE'S A CRITIC

Critics will often sway your perception with their subtle contributions to your life. Take into account if the criticism is worth the horse it rode in on. Some criticism is good, but sometimes it is not for you. Some criticism has been put out there to de-rail you. Be careful who you allow to shape your perception, ideas or dreams.

Everyone is not meant to mold you or be a voice in your developmental stages of life. Use the sense that God gave you on who and what to listen to. Weigh your options. Discern motives. And then make your decision on whether or not you will use the information given to you.

The bible says in **1 Timothy 6:20 NKJV**, *"O Timothy! Guard what was committed to your trust, avoiding the profane and idle babblings and contradictions of what is falsely called knowledge—"*

Some people will just speak to you concerning your destiny without any careful consideration of what they have left you with concerning your precious life. Then there you are trying to put the pieces of the hope you had back together before they spilled their thoughtless advice all over you. This is so important.

In this journey we call life we must develop a "know how" of what to listen to and what not to listen to. Discern from jump street if this is something that you need or want to listen to. Does the advice belong to you or someone else, because even some things that sound good to your ears may not be for you. Ask yourself these simple questions:

IN THE BEGINNING

> 1. Does this person love you enough to tell you the truth?
> 2. Are they advising you to help themselves, you or both?
> 3. What vein is the criticism coming out of? Love, anger, pain or help.
> 4. Does the advice build you up or tear you down?

Think these things over before, during and after taking advice from someone. In the beginning, even though I was a leader I allowed the wrong direction and criticism to steer my life resulting in a delay of my reaching the elevation in life I was meant to achieve in that season and this made me a follower.

Whoever seemed to know what they were talking about…there I was listening. But after I had had enough of the dead end contributions, I realized something had to change. Don't let this be your problem in the beginning.

BIG THINGS CAN COME IN SMALL PACKAGES

The bible asked the question in **Zechariah**

4:10a *"For who hath despised the day of small beginnings?"* I believe this is one of the primary places of defeat when starting a new work or going after your God given destiny and purpose. It's so easy to fall into the wrong mindset when you look around and realize how small your resources are. You begin to see that what you are working with appears to be too small for the job.

The people, equipment, education, connections and the big one…finances. We look at all these things and sometimes we allow it to incapacitate us and keep us from moving forward. You see I learned that in the small place is where God develops you the most. I perceive that God uses those small arenas to teach about the pre-destined place. If you don't have any quarrels with the people that no one knows then when you are facing those on the big stage in opposition you would never know how to fight. The small place is the practice ground for the big game.

I recall David whom when questioned about his ability to take on Goliath he referred to his victories when he was in the field with the sheep. To the natural eye and through human reasoning, in comparison to Goliath, David's victories with the lion and the bear were very small. But to David, those victories qualified him to take on Goliath. Those small victories in isolated places gave David the mentality that he could take on anybody, anywhere!

So we can't avoid the little starts and places in life because God is using them to sharpening us. Many want to connect with the well-known or the wealthy straight out of the gate but I've come to know that when you advance yourself to a level that you are not prepared for, you not only set yourself up for embarrassment but you also miss out on critical, key developmental phases that were put there to get you ready along the way.

What a shame it would be to get to a great place or stage and not know everything you need to know to occupy that level. It's not just getting there, its staying there and completing the job. This is why many come and go. They skipped stages and arrived to a place they could not maintain because they were not patient enough to endure the small place and beginnings which are assigned to us all.

WHAT'S MONEY GOT TO DO WITH IT?

Let's deal with one issue we all will

encounter no matter what level we are on and that's the matter of finances. When beginning a project, working a plan or setting a goal, finances will inevitably play a role of some kind.

I think back to how I paralyzed myself and hindered my progress because I did not have the money I needed or at times wanted to complete the task at hand. There were times when if I just did enough leg work, finances did not matter.

If you stop moving forward to wait until money is there then you may miss key opportunities for God to activate favor toward you in the situation. I can recall on several occasions where it looked grim and because I didn't cease to trust God for provision and didn't look at what I didn't have, what I had ended up being enough to get the job done.

Now don't get me wrong there are times when the right capital is needed and without it you frustrate your efforts. Discern whether God is challenging you in faith to trust him for the results or if He is saying trust him for the tangible dollar.

You may also have the people alongside to help but may need wisdom on how to get the people you have to produce the results according to your vision. If you don't assemble the people you have with much prayer and wait on those that are obviously qualified then you may miss God showing how he truly can take a small beginning and put his hand on it to produce the desired result.

You should know the bigger the job surely the bigger the budget. So your faith shall be lifted to believe God for a substantial amount of finances to ensure you are in position to see your faith manifested in the dimension you are believing for.

For the bigger venture finances certainly need to be outlined and solidified.

The beginning stages is deciphering whether you go forward with or without certain instrumental things in order to move yourself and vision into the place of manifestation. Know the difference.

If God is saying wait that's all you need to know. Wait means wait and if finances are the issue then he is saying wait till I provide the necessary funds to complete the task in the beginning.

CHAPTER 2

BUILDING CONFIDENCE

Most potential is never developed because of a lack of confidence. Some people never take that initial step needed to begin. Self-confidence is needed, for example, when contemplating trying out for the basketball, football, soccer, band or baseball teams.

Without the confidence to step out you will remain in your current condition wondering what could have been. Some professional athletes did not play sports in middle school or elementary school and didn't decide to try-out for the team until 10th or 11th grades.

Somewhere inside themselves they discovered they had the needed confidence in their abilities to make the team despite their past lack of experience. You might be surprised at what a simple "*I can do this*" or to hear, "*You can do this*," can do to build your confidence. Or they believed what the Word of God had to say on the matter through the Apostle Paul in **Philippians 4:13 NKJV** which states, "*I can do all things through Christ who strengthens me.*" What do you believe? It matters. What you believe could mean the difference between you becoming one of the greats being cheered on by the crowd or just being a spectator always cheering from the sidelines wondering what could have been. It is my hope that after reading this chapter this will not be your story.

I could give you some statistics, a pie graph or give you some psychological insight of how a lack of confidence can paralyze your advancement in life. But I choose to speak from my heart and my own experiences on this one.

As I mentioned in Chapter One, it seemed to me as if I lacked something in life that others in my family possessed. So when I compared myself to others, I was unable to flourish because of my lack of confidence in the skills and abilities God had given me. It is one thing to discover a gift, but it is another to be confident in your gift. Confidence takes the gift to another level.

Confidence causes your gift(s) to soar to new heights and levels all because it was applied. Becoming confident in my ability or potential, not only gave me an opportunity to advance but I also affected those around me who had not yet activated their confidence.

Will your legacy be that people will talk about what you could have done with your life if only you had the confidence in yourself to see what other saw? Will they say that you were always on the verge of greatness but allowed fear to hold you hostage to achieving your full potential?

You can decide today to believe in yourself. No one can do it for you and no one can walk through the doors of opportunity that have your name on them…but YOU!

YOU ARE NOT ALONE

Accept the challenges in life without fear and doubt knowing that God will see you through to the next level. If you fail, learn from it and build on that and continue to make your way to your destiny. Without faith it is impossible to please God (**Hebrews 11:6a,** but with God the impossible is possible!! (see **Matthew 19:26** and **Mark 10:27**)

Moses lacked confidence because he did not speak eloquently. So God had to build his confidence in the power and resources that he had already given him to bring the children of Israel out of Egypt, a land of bondage.

Confidence in yourself will not only determine whether *you* come out, but an entire generation is riding on you fulfilling your purpose and destiny. Will you take the steps to building up your confidence? Do you realize that your breakthrough into the unlimited blessings of God are dependent upon on you being confident enough in God to step out of your comfort zone? If we were, I believe that most of us would move.

The question is, "Do you believe there are unlimited blessings waiting on you? We need to put our confidence not only in our abilities but in the creator of the ability and once we do that you will surely see the hand of God. Confidence is not only predicated on what you can do, but what God can do. Do you not know that your abilities are limited but his abilities are unlimited?

Trust in God that He knows what He is doing by using your average, good or great ability that he has placed in you because ultimately he has a purpose for it no matter how big or small it may seem.

Confidence is essential. The little things make a big difference. If God said it then it's done. If the Lord of the universe has spoken a word into your life whether through someone or directly, that should be enough to gain confidence from.

Meditate on his prophetic words spoken

unto you with all surety. Document them and hold on to them until they come to pass. God is not like man that he should lie. See **Numbers 23:19**.

So in your attempts to accomplish purpose and destiny know that it is already done just because he said it. God does not speak in vain or for not. **1 Samuel 15:29 NIV**, "*He who is the Glory of Israel does not lie or change his mind; for he is not a man, that he should change his mind."*

He speaks to bring you into the knowledge of the fact that he has already done it. Just know. He speaks to us to let us know there is hope despite the fact that we can't see what he is doing. He speaks to confirm what he has already spoken to your spirit. He speaks to prepare you for the next season or level that God is about to bring you into. Be aware of your confidence builders. Be aware of your moments of clarity because they will take you a long way.

Build confidence in others. Don't be afraid to encourage others despite your short comings or lack thereof. Sometimes people just need a push from an outside source. Keep an open eye out for individuals who need encouragement. It is our duty as believers and a privilege as human beings to develop a strong character for helping others. After you have found confidence in yourself, move further to share what you have discovered. That is the main reason for your discovery.

Confidence within yourself can make or break you. I noticed that people who have great determination are normally those of little or minimum talent. Time after time we wonder where all the talent is. Well I will tell you. The majority of truly talented people are somewhere struggling with their confidence. Sometimes a person's gift can be so great that it overwhelms them and they have no idea how to operate in such greatness bestowed upon them.

There are times others have seen the greatness on them and have made it a point to tear them down and it damaged their confidence. It's tough being extremely gifted and not have the right people and personalities around you to cultivate it and bring it out.

Most people's gifts go to waste because of others that didn't recognize it or because insecure people that wanted to hide or undermine the gifts inside.

Ask yourself…"Have I lost my confidence?" More than likely it happens when confronted or combated by jealous or envious people. These type of people are normally live with a lack of confidence in themselves so it will be difficult to have it for someone else.

Allow me to share a wonderful quote that I believe sums it up best…" *"When you're different, sometimes you don't see the millions of people who accept you for what you are. All you notice is the person who doesn't."* — **Jodi Picoult**

Unfortunately we don't have the choice as children to choose who grooms us for greatness. So often times this discovery of a lack of confidence is way too late. Maybe today I have caught you at the right time. Today I want to speak to you and encourage that you still can reach your goals! All you got to do is step into confidence. I know your saying "How do I do that?" Well, I'm glad you asked.

BUILDING BLOCKS OF CONFIDENCE

Romans 12:2 NKJV states, *"And do not be conformed to this world, but be transformed by the renewing of your mind, that you may prove what is that good and acceptable and perfect will of God.*

The primary building block to confidence

BUILDING CONFIDENCE

is your thinking (consciously, subconsciously and learned patterns of processing information.)

In order to accomplish the perfect will of God for our lives we must have transformational thinking in all areas of our lives. Changing our thinking and replacing insecurity for confidence can shift you very easily into a different dimension in your life.

Everyone has a place in their life where they have the confidence they need. Maybe your confident might be in your style of dress or maybe your confident is in your speech but lack the confidence needed when you are put to the test in other areas. Well look at this. That same confidence you have in the area of dress or speech can be applied in the other areas if you just change your mind about it and realize it's all the same principle.

YOU CAN DO IT!

The infamous one-liner..."*You Can Do It*" echoes throughout the 1998 American sports/comedy film, *The Waterboy*, where Adam Sandler's character, Bobby Boucher cheers on the players of the fictitious football team inciting them to believe in themselves and each other. As you begin to have full trust in and reliance on God and His Word…you can do it…whatever *it* is for your life.

I recall being on the varsity basketball team in the 11th grade and as we practiced and interacted with one another, I recognized that I had the ability to lead this team as the point guard. One day we were practicing and I was challenged by one of the seniors on my own team during the five-on-five pick-up game.

As we played, I begin to see that he was threatened by me because every time I had the ball or was playing defense on him he began to taunt me verbally. As the game play went on I allowed what he was saying and not what he was actually doing on the court to get into my head. This resulted in a break in my focus and was a hard hit to my confidence.

I was more concerned with the things he was saying and not seeing that my ability matched his and beyond. I left day after day confused, disappointed and ultimately defeated because I allowed what he was saying to transform the way I saw myself and my abilities…but in the wrong direction.

One day during practice I made it up in my mind that no matter what he said or did I was

BUILDING CONFIDENCE

going to give him the business. As we played he made his usual comments about my game but I didn't take anything he was saying into consideration. I continued to play pressure defense and attacked on offense and as the game went on I saw this puzzled look on his face.

He couldn't figure out why he wasn't getting to me. It eventually affected him because he was used to taking me off my game with his words. I locked out every negative word and relied on my ability and focus to give me the edge. When I became confident in my abilities and didn't feed into the attack on my focus, I was able to hold my own on the court.

The following season I became the starting point guard and captain at 5'10" in height but I had the confidence of a 6"5" shooting guard. My change came when I just believed more in what I could do and didn't allow outside influences to dictate how well I would play the game.

Confidence is everything. Was I the best? No. Was I the best for the job? Yes. Simply because I had more confidence in my ability than the rest of the candidates.

I can honestly say I wasn't the most athletic guy in the whole school, but I was definitely the most confident on the court. After that experience I developed the type of confidence to take on anyone on any skill level. I decided that I would not allow what was spoken to me or of me to dictate my performance.

Fear is the main agent that cripples you and leaves you with no confidence. The fear of embarrassment, under achievement or inadequacy are enemies to your confidence and destiny!

Because of these fears you perform poorly if at all. Confidence also affects your motivation to begin something new or even continue in a work you started but slacked off in. You think you just don't feel like it or you are too tired perhaps to complete it, when in actuality, you have lost confidence in yourself to complete the task at hand.

Many of us have little knowledge of what God has placed in us and because of that we don't have confidence in the places that we should and need to.

Spending time in a quiet place in prayer and searching the heart of God for insight on what he has placed in you is a good start to knowing what God has stored in you. Once he reveals to you the unique gifts that he has placed in you, you can began the journey of cultivating

BUILDING CONFIDENCE

the greatness in you. If you stick with this process of transforming your mind to the will of God, an automatic increase in confidence will come.

CHAPTER 3

YOU CAN BE THE BEST TOO

In a world where there are so many great men and women it can be difficult to find your place in all of this. You can be admiring someone from a distance or you could be very close to someone that is accomplishing and/or doing great things.

In your observing you can't allow someone else's success to drown out the voice that's calling you to greatness or allow your own vision to become blurry because of all the wonderful things that are on display before you. It is true that you can find yourself spectating and lose all focus of who you are and what it is that you are to achieve in life.

Greatness is all around us, in us and a part of us but we must be aware of the things that we are experiencing and without allowing the experiences of others to stagnate us from becoming fruitful ourselves.

For instance, many of us are fighting within ourselves as well as others to bring forth the great calling that is within us. In life you will attract others of like traits and ideas. Be aware not

YOU CAN BE THE BEST TOO

to find yourself on a boat that will not dock in a place where you need to get off and explore the island of greatness on your own.

What am I trying to say? The majority of the human population are spectators because at some point they settled for being a part of someone else success instead of giving birth to their own baby.

They became cheerleaders of a game that they are supposed to be playing in. When do you ever try-out for the team? When do you ever sharpen your skills enough to get in the game or make the starting line-up? Granted, every one can't be a star player but those of us who are, have to be mindful of who we are and do whatever it takes to bring out all that is within us.

Don't settle for second best. Jesus said "Greater works will you do than I." What a powerful statement from someone that had done such great exploits. Even He knew that your experience with Him should be put to greater use. I know that He is to be honored and this we definitely should do. But don't get so stuck on what you read that you never allow those words to lift from the pages and become real in your life.

Damion Jones

You can do great things too! Even if you are under great leadership. You don't always have to limit yourself because of someone else's success makes it appear to be an insurmountable task to be the best you. Greater works you shall do. You can be the best too!

There are people that are poised to do something extraordinary. Unfortunately, somewhere along the line they became satisfied with watching others accomplish their hopes and dreams. Never again to take thought that there is something greater calling them in the distance and because of a deaf ear they can no longer hear the cry of greatness beckoning for a response.

Don't get me wrong it's perfectly fine to help escort others into their destinies. By all means, giving of yourself is a great thing. But don't forget about yourself and your life's purpose that you are responsible for fulfilling. You must be in tune enough to know what it is you should be doing in all of this and when is it time for you to focus on the things that so deeply penetrate your thought process. We know that serving or the giving of ourselves is an important step toward greatness.

Most people that have achieved great things often testify of sitting at the feet of

YOU CAN BE THE BEST TOO

someone else who shared their wisdom with them. So I am not telling you to bypass your season of learning and preparation. This is a much needed thing. I eagerly encourage you to get the most out of your mentors. Just be mindful enough to know when it is time for you to leave the nest. One day you must fly on your own without coaching or direct assistance from a second party.

Greatness requires you at times to step out into unchartered territory. You have to make up in your mind that you can do great things too. Don't get stuck pondering your thoughts in an endless struggle to make up your mind on whether or not to become great.

Wouldn't it be great to fulfill your dreams? Wouldn't it be even greater to fulfill your destiny and purpose? Are you doing what God put you on this earth to do? Are you even on track to accomplishing some of the things that God has placed in your heart to do?

If your answer to any of these questions is "no", then you may need to re-evaluate your life.

There is nothing more fulfilling than being everything that God has purposed you to do. That is the place where you will release the weight of life's hardships. That is the place (the will of God for your life) where you will soar. You see, I didn't know my purpose until I was about 22 years old. I would try different things to find validation in life. I would hang around all types of people just to find a way to relate.

Unfortunately, I never found what I was looking for in those dark and lonely attempts to be noticed or validated. But when I stepped into true destiny and purpose I could see that everything I was looking for on the outside was already in me just waiting to be explored, experienced and shared.

In those places, I live freely because that is what I was created for. His purpose…not my own or someone else's label. So greatness is not found on the outside it is actually on the inside of you.

The bible says in **1 John 4:4 KJV,** *"Ye are of God, little children, and have overcome them: because greater is he that is in you, than he that is in the world."*

There is a force that is inside of us that empowers us beyond are human capabilities. It gives us the power to become great. Tap in! You can be great too!

CHAPTER 4

YOUR RELATIONSHIPS: DO THEY HELP OR HINDER?

Being in relationship with other people is part of our daily lives whether we like it or not. Some people are in our lives because of someone else or because of your direct consent. Some people are in your life because you have not put them out and shut the door behind them.

These people continue to hang around until you take control of the situation. I chose this particular topic in this chapter because it is important to take notice of the type of relationships you build as God elevates your life.

Relationships with people that are in your life can determine how far you will go. You always hear people talking about building healthy relationships. It took me a while to realize that the relationships you have with people in your life matter a great deal. The stronger the relationship the more you can achieve in the relationship.

Let me start out by talking about relationships that hinder. The relationships that hinder are the ones that bring you down when you are in the presence of that person or replay negative words they may have said. Do you have a friend that is always negative? Do they always say discouraging things to you and about you? Does this person never seem to get beyond the negative things in life? Normally this person does not get a lot accomplished.

If they do they never get gratification out of the accomplishment. They always find something wrong with what they are doing or what someone else is doing. I'm sorry to inform you of this but this is a hindering relationship.

This person normally draws on other people's weaknesses. When you leave their presence you generally leave drained and depressed, not motivated and uplifted. This relationship is hindering you from a fulfilling life, blocking you and depriving you of a positive outlook on life.

This person needs to be driven to a dead end and left right there. I'm just kidding, but on the real, this relationship may rob you of some victories that you may be about to embark upon. When you get the victory they will come and suck the life out of the celebration by seeking to point out a deficit in the victory. Sort of like a reporter who tells a story about a big championship victory but can't help but call attention to a bad quarter or play to frustrate the MVP or player of the game to take their focus off of the great celebration they are already engaged in. Kick this person to the curb! (Not literally, of course.)

      I have had people in my life like that and all I did was walk away…Never to return to the graveyard of negativity. I may see them somewhere and I will be cordial and speak and keep on going. While its safe to say that people do change, grow and mature, in most cases, if you open the door for them to come in they may pick up where they left off and you definitely don't want that so be sure to seek the Holy Spirit for discernment and understanding. This could also be an opportunity to operate in forgiveness and compassion. But if you are led to close the door and lock it and throw away the key in the sea of forgetfulness…do it!

      Sounds easier than it is doesn't it? As you progress upon your journey to ascend to your respective point of elevation you will encounter people who are jealous and find validation by knocking everyone else down to make them feel better about themselves.

      Jealousy is cruel like the grave. The jealousy of others can affect your life's progress if you allow these type of individuals to be a part of your life. They will be a hindrance, a weight. Even if it doesn't stop you, it definitely can slow you down. It would be alright for you, at this point, to begin to evaluate the people that fit this description. Many will be those who are closest to you. Are they helping or hindering? This makes it even harder to separate yourself from the negative forces.

THOUGHTS ARE POWERFUL

Another category of hindering relationships is that or those who aren't quite so vocal with their negativity. They hold there negativity to themselves but silently crush you with foul thoughts that crowd your atmosphere. Did you know thoughts have a presence?

They don't talk much but you can undoubtedly feel their negative vibe when you are around them. They can sometimes be worse than the first description because they seek to kill you silently. These people can only be detected by your spiritual radar. When they come into your presence they may not say anything but you sure feel the negativity in the air. Normally, these people will smile in your face but in the back of their minds they are destroying your every move…piece by piece.

Silent negativity. Not heard, but felt. These people are dangerous because they will have had an opportunity to speak up about an issue to save you grief or suffering and choose not to in order see you fail.

They will see the cliff coming and instead of yelling out a warning, they will sit in the seat with the best view of your failure and watch you walk yourself into pure defeat without warning.

The negativity is so deeply rooted in them that seeing you flop is better than helping you elevate to the next level. There are times when you need people to show you the error in your ways but someone who doesn't contribute anything but negative thoughts concerning your elevation is a problem will need to be eliminated out of your life.

Let me ask you a question. Are you allowing the presence of a negative person to hang around you when you know in your gut they are there just to trip you up?

Most of us recognize unwanted relationships in our lives, but do we ever do anything about it? Are you bold enough to tell that unwanted influence to stop calling or to stop coming by to visit. What is stopping you from taking control of your relationships and making sure they are healthy ones? You will find that if you remove these toxic relationships, things will go a lot smoother and you will be less weighed down by the pressure of a hindering relationship.

THE POWER OF POSITIVE CONNECTIONS

Let's take a minute to focus on relationships that help your elevation. Of course they can be hard to find but you know they are out there. A relationship that helps you fulfill your God given purpose is like a cold glass of water in 105° temperature in Texas. Downright refreshing.

There's nothing like having a person in your life that doesn't mind encouraging you to become the best that you can be. A positive relationship should consist of love, patience, understanding and accountability. Do you have someone in your life that loves you beyond your faults? This person or persons see past your mood swings and dysfunctions and will nurture you back to your position of elevation. They will be patient with you when you are not quite where you should be or you have not matured in an area where they have.

They will have a certain level of understanding for who you are, where you have come from and where you are going. They will be able to understand your passion for elevation. Last, but not least, they will have hold you accountable for your actions. If they care about you and your life they will make sure you keep your commitments.

They will hold you to your word regardless of the circumstances. Accountability is important in a positive, helpful relationship that helps keep you on schedule.

These are just some nuggets for you to consider. Begin to look for these traits in your relationships and I promise you will begin to see things different at your point of elevation.

CHAPTER 5

DESTINY KILLERS

Drugs and Alcohol came in to my life at a very early. I was introduced to marijuana at the age of twelve. The focus of this chapter is to show you how it cripples your elevation. Drugs can really alter your sense of perception and truth.

As I began to smoke, a fantasy land developed in my mind about life. At first, I felt guilty for being so young. Then I would just do it to fit in with a certain group of friends that were addicts.

One night while heavily under the influence, they turned on me and tried to beat me up…but that's another story altogether. There's so much that goes on in the life of the user (or abuser) that it is even hard for me to stay focused on my main topic.

From that early exposure I lived an existence that allowed me to escape my world in a two inch piece of paper filled with a mind altering substance that only God can truly deliver a person from.

Throughout high school I would use periodically during the week and mostly on the weekends. When I would indulge, I would be in another world. Whatever my problems were, they didn't exist during that period of time. This habit hindered my growth spiritually and there's no measuring the mental effects it had on me. It took my focus off of God and it literally became a god in my life.

It caused me to treat women differently and the people that loved me. It all started by the influence of another person. When I first began using, it didn't seem to affect me the way people said it would. However, over a period of time, I became a different person. By the time I was eighteen years of age I was using regularly. This initiated a downhill spiral of depression, failure, and bad decisions.

Elevation was not possible for me at this particular time in my life because I was too consumed with a false altitude. I thought I was elevated but I was only lying to myself. I Tricked myself into believing I was something more when I got high or drunk…but I was only numbing the pain of my true reality.

That reality I convinced myself of was that I was a loser and a disappointment to my family. But the drugs talked really sweet to my ears and told me I was somebody because of the way it made me feel.

You see, when I speak of elevation most people automatically think financially, materialistically or in a notoriety spectrum. However, the elevation that I am speaking of is spiritual. Growing as a person of purpose and destiny.

Drugs and alcohol hinder your progress and will totally alter your direction in your spiritual life. It takes your focus off of making good decisions. When consumed in excess, it beats away at your house of preparation only to merely blow it down in the end.

Some people use drugs and other inhibitors, moderately. Some people drink reasonably and that is okay with them. I choose to refrain 24 hours a day, 7 days a week, 365 days a year in order to elevate to who I am to become.

You see people who appear to be successful by what they have like cars, houses, boats or connections are not always having success within themselves. You have but only to read the news or search the internet for story after story of how the "rich and famous" are not always so happy.

The majority of them can't handle themselves as a person in any given circumstance.

How much more if they are drunk or high?

STIMULATIONS THAT
THWART ELEVATION

    You may be a user and things are going fine for you…it seems. Believe me, the experiment that you are doing on yourself is definitely eating away at you surely and slowly. It creeps up like a thief in the night only to steal something so precious from you.

    One in this situation may experience unforeseen road block; all hell begins to break loose and nothing seems to go right. A wreck that keeps you from getting home for dinner on time. Rush hour traffic that is only caused by on-lookers of a car on the side of the road. A police that stops you for no reason and you're on your way to an important meeting. A child support case that comes through the mail from a girl you never had sex with. Locking your keys in the car and you're in a bad neighborhood and your cell phone is in the car.

    These are minor comparisons to putting a gun to your head or your brain being roasted frying in a frying pan of harmful chemicals. How about having your liver dipped in poison? Better yet, having your head stuck in a box of smoke and no one will help you out. How about waking up in one of the games from the film, "Saw?"

It starts out as a mere cigarette every now and then and the next thing you know, you are participated in a "joint" passing frenzy. In a short time, you're a regular buyer and eventually, you're smoking every day because your problems are outweighing your solutions.

Because of your use, life hardens and now you realize you're not getting as high as you did when you first started. The realization of this leads you to trying even heavier drugs like cocaine or methamphetamines. Keep in mind these particular drugs are more addictive. So now your elevation is paralyzed by a substance that is controlling your mind.

Whoa! It all started with just a cigarette a day that couldn't take the pain away. This illustration is not even the half of it. There's so much more that goes on behind the scenes and behind the closed doors many think are so private.

If you have found yourself under any of these circumstances may I suggest you visit your local church to get spiritual help for what is certainly a spiritual battle. Discovering the heart of God for you and your life is the number one way out of your dilemma. The longer you stay there the deeper you will sink. Only God's loving arms are long enough to pull you out of that pit you will eventually be in or are already standing in.

As I recognize my decrease as an elevated being it frustrated me. I wanted to overcome these addictions. I had to realize my answers were not in people, places or things. My answers are and were in my Lord and Savior Jesus Christ. He delivered me when I surrendered my will to His.

Will you be courageous enough to do the same despite what your friends will say or how people will treat you after your decision to elevate from the place where you are?

It's been fourteen years since my use. It's so much better on this level of sobriety. In an upcoming book dedicated to my victory and deliverance from substance abuse, I will tell you about all the wonderful things that have transpired since my decision to elevate. Going from substance control to spiritual guidance being led by what and Who is Real.

I overcame a phony since of security while diving head and heart first into the safety of the arms of my Savior Jesus Christ. My life is better now that I can think clearer and make sound decisions. Remember no one is perfect, but you are much better off sober. God bless at that point of elevation.

CHAPTER 6

TIRED

    The journey to elevation can be very fulfilling as well as physically and mentally draining. Imagine what it must feel like for a seasoned mountain climber to ascend to the top of the tallest mountain in the world, Mount Everest. How much stamina, courage, drive and determination do you think is required to successfully make this climb?

    What physical and mental shape do you believe the climber must be in to arrive safely at his or her destination?

    The feelings that you are left with from going up and down the hills, mountains and valleys of experience can be hard to balance at times. Of course it's not as hard to find the energy to continue on this never ending journey when you experience triumph.

    The Bible gives us clear answers for obtaining the balance we need in text such as, **Isaiah 41:13 ESV**, *"For I, the Lord your God, hold your right hand; it is I who say to you, "Fear not, I am the one who helps you."* and **John 5:30 ESV**, *"I can do nothing on my own. As*

TIRED

I hear, I judge, and my judgment is just, because I seek not my own will but the will of him who sent me."

When you experience victory in your walk of life it is much easier to get out of bed and face the next challenge. You smile more. You're more giving than normal and you are a much better person to deal with, I hope. Somehow music sounds more appealing. Your favorite songs seem to ring off inside of you unannounced. The same steak you had when you couldn't' see your way is savored with every bite after a victory.

So why is that everything in life seems so much better when we are having a mountain top experience? Is it that our perception is better. It seems somewhat selfish to only find gratitude in life when things are going your way. It is my hope with this chapter that I could somehow show you that despite the fact that things will not always go your way you can still enjoy life to the fullest.

The definition of elevate in the Webster is simply stated, "to lift up or raise; to promote to a higher rank."   In life you will grow tired despite the victories or defeats. When we are tired is when we are the most vulnerable. We tend to take things for granted when we don't feel quite up to the challenges that life has thrown at us. Believe me life doesn't ease up just because we are tired. Life doesn't' slow down so we can catch up and regain strength.

This world would probably be a much better place if every time you had money problems the bill collectors waited until you got your finances in order before they expected payment. In reality, the bills keep coming and you have to find a way to pay them or they will report you to the credit bureau.

My point is that in life you will have opportunities to grow weary. Regardless of whether or not you are up to the challenge you must produce even when you are tired.

Being tired can ultimately lead to unfinished business. The bible says be not weary in well doing cause in due season you shall reap if you don't quit, faint, or give up. (**See Galatians 6:9**)

I defined elevate for you earlier to show you that elevation is merely rising up higher than where you are. When feeling tired or weary it is essential to have the ability to elevate beyond your tiredness. This one area in life must be handled carefully because it could make or break you. Don't let your contribution to life drain you

TIRED

and leave you unproductive. If you need a break, take a vacation, but don't allow yourself to become so tired that it causes you to become a wreck. Get the proper rest needed to produce on the level you need to produce. Find ways to regain your strength. Meditate, get a massage, get in the hot tub, listen to music that soothes you.

Do whatever replenishes you as a being so you will not run out of creative energy when it is most needed. You may not necessarily be in a place where you can change your job, who you work for or where you live. You may just be tired of where you are in life. Perhaps your current position has grown and there seems to be no signs of change coming.

Remember elevation is first spiritual. Life doesn't get better around you until it first gets better within you. You just make a decision to work with what is around you. We tend to associate better life with better living and that is not
always true. You can have a mansion and all the amenities, but if you have no friends or love ones to share it with you are no better off than someone on skid row.

It's not what you have it's how you live. You can choose today to enjoy your life just the way it is if you lift up or raise your level of thinking and perception. Your surroundings haven't change but you sure did.

Things may not always change around us but we can always change the way we feel. Whether you feel tired weary or just down right discouraged, remember you have the ability inside of you to feel any way you want. For example, most of my life.

Between ages 19-22 I waited tables with shifts that started between 10 or 11 in the morning. At the age of about 25 I had a job as a restaurant manager that required me to be in at 6a.m.

The training was about twenty minutes from my house and during that time we still did not have to be in until 10 o'clock. After the training was over they placed me in one of the franchise stores as an assistant to the general manager of that store. The only catch was the store was located one hour from my house. Oh boy! I had to be in at six so that means I had to be up at 4:30 in the morning just to be at work on time.

This was the earliest I ever had to rise for a job. Yes, I was definitely being elevated in position, but I had to change my attitude towards

TIRED

waking up so early. Not only that, but twice a week I had to unload and stock products from a diesel truck that was waiting on me when I arrived to work. This was no easy task, especially when someone called in from the evening shift and I had to work that shift too!

    Talk about being tired. That meant I got off at 12 o'clock, made the hour long drive home, showered before retiring to bed and had to be right back up at 4:30am to do it all over again. It wasn't long before I was feeling the effects of a lack of sleep.

    The bible said His strength is made perfect in your time of weakness. (**See 2 Corinthians 12:9)**

    Through it all I found the strength to be on time. I found the strength to do my job no matter how the day went. We even made bonus at that store for the first time in ten months the first two months I was there. Sales were up and everybody was happy. It wasn't long before my work ethic caused my name to be on the lips of the owners. I made a decision within myself to change my attitude and not dwell on the fact that I didn't like waking up so early and trained my mind to see the situation through Gods eyes. I realized that He was going to get me through. His strength became my strength and I eventually made it through. I overcame having a defeated, tired and weary soul and went on to start my own business.

In changing my outlook God was able to use that experience to train me to one day work for myself. I changed my outlook and God changed my destiny. So I say to you that are tired or at a crossroad in your life if you beat your weariness and change your mental attitude your point of elevation may be closer than you think.

The point of elevation is a perspective and not always a literal place. It's having a viewpoint that is from Heaven downward…a view from the top as it were. Thinking beyond where you are even when your physical body is limited. Allow your mind to take you to the unlimited realm of the spirit and to help you reach your destiny in God and the Kingdom.

CHAPTER 7

TESTING GROUND

I have been in many peculiar situations in my life. Many trials and storms have beat up against my house of hope. There are times when I wonder how I have made it through the trials. There are things in life that can happen to you that you have no explanation for.

You will not know how you got in the situation and you will not know how to come out. One thing I know now is that God is definitely with me. The only answer I have is he has brought me through. Webster defines the word test as an exam, trial, quiz, analyze, verify or validate. As I look back over my life the testing point has not been as successful as I have wanted it to be.

One thing I realized is that if you fail a test over and over again, it will come around again. Even if you pass remember the lesson you learned because you may need that same information on the next test. So why does God

TESTING GROUND

test us? [1]When we ask why God tests us, or allows us to be tested, we are admitting that testing does indeed come from Him, as clearly taught in Scripture. Although we are forbidden to test Him (Deuteronomy 6:16; Matthew 4:7), when God tests His children, He does a valuable thing. David sought God's testing, asking Him to examine his heart and mind and see that they were true to Him (Psalm 26:2; 139:23). In both the Old and New Testaments, the words translated "test" mean to prove by trial.

Therefore, when God tests His children, the purpose is to prove that our faith is real. Not that God needs to prove it to Himself since He knows all things; rather, He is proving to us that our faith is real, that we are truly His children, and that no trial or test will overcome that faith. In school tests are taken to determine your level of understanding, maturity and qualifications. Some are taken to bring at the end of a class. So it is in life I believe--we are tested daily or periodically just to see where are hearts really are. I believe tests are there to discern your motives.

They also are there to purify you. As God

elevates us in life I believe test are very much in order. I can remember being tested with money. I have worked on jobs that have presented opportunities for me to steal money from the company. The fact that I was honest and showed integrity revealed something about my character and the God that I serve.

On that same job I received promotion after promotion but it was the passing of the test that paved the way for a new opportunity. Passing the test was the difference between getting fired or being promoted. I haven't passed all my tests, of course. For instance, I recall a time I was a waiter and I aspired to be in a management position with a particular certain restaurant chain.

I shared my desire with my then superior and let him know of my goal to be a manager. From that point on, he began to watch me closer. He began a series of tests to see if I was ready for that position. The first thing he did was ask me to perform above that of my regular duties as outlined in my job description…some of which caused me to have to work later hours and supervise and monitor other employees. After passing the initial test, he raised the stakes. The restaurant where I worked was a training facility for managers. One day he asked me to start coming in early to start training other would be managers.

Bear in mind, not only am I not a morning person, I was being asked to train others for a position that I wanted. Soon afterward, I arrived in time for my regular shift…not early, as my superior has requested. When he inquired as to my tardiness, it was then that I remembered his request…this was the day I was to train the managers.

I believe that my internal attitude about training others for a position I desired clouded my judgment and led to me lose focus on the very task that could have opened the door for me. Unfortunately, from that day forward I was never asked to train again. Instead, they offered the opportunity to a colleague who accepted the challenge and was at the top of her game. She was eventually promoted to the corporate office.

As for me, I eventually sought out other employment. The moral of the story is because I did not pass the test that was given to me I missed my opportunity to be promoted. In life you will be tested. You must be ready and willing to do what it takes to pass.

Your life may depend on it. I struggled through so many jobs after that until I got the lesson. In life you will ultimately take the same test over and over again until you pass. Why not get the lesson so you can get the blessing? Realize that there is something that God wants you to see before He will open the next door. If you are stuck in one place and you seem to be going around in circles.

Maybe it is because you keep failing the test. If you keep doing the same thing you will keep getting the same result. If you want to be successful in your relationships, but you can't seem to be faithful, how in the world will you accomplish that?

TESTING GROUND

If you are tested in this area will you deny yourself so you can move into victory in that relationship? Or will you fail and end up running from person to person? Constantly failing the test and ruining all of your relationships. Make the decision today to be faithful. The passing of the test will determine whether you elevate into a beautiful relationship set aside by God with one person under covenant.

Can you stand to be blessed? Well, pass the test! Finding fulfillment in certain areas in your life is simply determined by you making up your mind to do your homework, study, and pass the test. A single test could be the difference between you and your next level. God tested Abraham by asking him to sacrifice his son. I believe the Lord knew all along that he was not going to have him go through with it, but the test proved the pureness of his heart towards God.

The test determined whether he would become the father of many nations. The mountain top test qualified him for his next level. The higher the level the bigger the test. You may be called to oversee people one day, but your test may come through your servanthood. Your test results will determine how soon you are promoted.

When on the testing ground of life these tests will present themselves in many different ways. Your boss may test you. Your pastor may test you. Your spouse will test. Your children will test you and most assuredly, God will test you.

More than likely he will probably use all of the above to deliver the test. Please be aware of your test because whether or not you pass or fail will determine if you elevate to the next level.

CHAPTER 8

TRANSITION

In the transitional seasons of your life things may be a bit discombobulating to you. For one you're not where you were, but you have not arrived to the next place of destiny either. Even though physically we may be there, transition is still taking place in our minds.

I mean we try our best to keep up with God, but there are times he shifts you to a place ,turns your life upside down and it takes you some time to catch up mentally. Your surroundings are not the same. The way that you used to look at yourself you don't look at yourself the same way.

You have discovered something different in your life and the adjustment period has begun. In the midst of tragedy God has begun to push you into destiny. You have went from destruction to decision and about to enter blessing. You are in transition. If this is where you are then it is you I want to talk to you right now.

The Children of Israel had been brought out of bondage and suddenly they found themselves in the wilderness and ended up staying there too long because they did not access the transition properly. I believe one of the main reasons why they stayed in the wilderness so long is because of their lack of understanding for the transition.

Between Egypt and the promise land there was a transitional period. It was an uncalculated situation that grew into a problem instead of a taxi cab to the land flowing with milk and honey. The transitional periods of your life are put there to prepare you for your next level. In between the past and the future is a transition that has been put there to shave off all the things that don't belong in your next level and put in you or bring out of you what is needed to abide on the next level.

The transition is never guaranteed to be smooth unless we praise him and have faith. Praise will sustain you and faith will take you through. Faith is the tenacity to stand through your transition or trial period until God brings you through. In the transitional period believing for your breakthrough is sometimes all you have.

You can't do it. You don't have the finances or the ability. All you have is God because everything else is unfamiliar. Before you were born God prepared a place for you called destiny and then put purpose in you to get there and right before you get to another level of manifest glory he begins to prepare you and in his preparation changes begin to happen around you that you did not calculate.

These changes are only set there to prepare you for your point of elevation. You are in transition. It's not that you're not going to get there you just have to be prepared for the next place. What happens to most people is in the transitional period they grow weary because of the process. There is not necessarily a time limit for transitions in your life or a way to measure what your being prepared for.

All you need to know is you're going to another level. The fact that I know change is coming is encouraging to me. I know that if I stay on course I will be where God wants me to be.

When going from one place in life to the other you will experience discomfort. Everything about you will be in the middle of a life shift. Your sleep, thoughts, relationships, work and quiet time will become uncomfortable during the transition. You will feel the effects of not being where you were, but you're not where you are going.

This place of change can be difficult for you because in this place in life you are aware of

TRANSITION

a tremendous change taking place in your life but you can't pin point the direction that God is taking your life in.

In this place you may feel like you are failing but in reality you're in the middle of being positioned for success. There is a good chance in this place you feel like you are stagnant or maybe even going backwards. Unusual thoughts of regret and defeat may come to your mind in this place because you are so shaken by not being in the old comfortable place.

You desire to move forward into a better place in life but you have miscalculated that the time would come for a change in your movement. You're moving now through the dark room. You can since that there is an exit. Your somewhere in the middle of this room making your way to the door the best way you can but your vision is impaired due to the dark season of transition in your life.

You're reaching for a door which is slightly out of reach due to the fact that you are standing close to the door of breakthrough but in the middle of passing through the room. You're in transition.

The agony of this place is that you know you are close to a change but yet you have no exact idea of when you will arrive to your next place. Responses of people bother you. Voices bother you. You even begin to bother yourself! You have stepped out of your old place of reside but have not arrived at your next destination. Matter of fact your somewhere in the middle. This must take place in your life.

You have to pass through this difficult place in your life in order to get to your next level. This shifty place is essential for your growth also. There will be many lessons finalized during this process to prepare you for your next place of operation.

There are times more than not that you will lose friendships in this place. In the transition is where you are challenged to make quick, precise changes that position you for your next dimension. There are some people close to you that will not understand your indifference but this must take place in order for you to transition to your next place.

If they don't stay in your life then they are not meant to be in your next season of elevation. Don't be afraid of this mysterious place. Courage is essential for you in this unfamiliar place.

Don't allow fear to grip you. You can't afford to be fearful or be distracted by what can

TRANSITION

or can't happen. Go in faith through the dark room of transition and only believe that what God has spoken will manifest after this transition which will cause you to arrive at the point of elevation.

Chapter 9

PASSION

By its very definition, passion means suffering. When you have determined in your heart that you are going to another level in your life we very seldom take into account the obstacles that may come our way that may cause us to suffer things like, pain from indifferent relatives or an unsupportive spouse.

Its almost 100 % guaranteed that we will run into issues along the way. There will be setbacks, delays and roadblocks. There will be times of frustration that make you wonder if you are on the right track. We always dream of the end result of our pursuit but we don't prepare for the things that so easily blind side us during our efforts to change.

You decide you're going to stop smoking but you didn't take into account that you would have withdrawals. You decided to stop drinking but never realized how it would affect your moods. You have given up partying and going to the club to fulfill your dream but forgot that you would be alone on Friday and Saturdays.

PASSION

You decide you're going to lose weight but underestimated the time it would take from your regular schedule to be in the gym on those painful days and nights.

When we make up our minds to go to another level in our life sometimes we overlook what it will cost us to be more. I can think of so many times I courageously stepped out to change and right in the middle of change I hit a wall that dazed me or I ran into some problems that I just don't know how to overcome.

Often times we find ourselves in predicaments that take more than just a decision to change. I recall when I began to feel the call to Pastor and start a church. All I could see was the end result. How great the services would be. How awesome the praise team would be. How packed the services would be because surely if He called me the people would just show up…right?

Well there has been a lot of work involved to produce the vision that was given to me. To be honest it has not been anything like I thought it would be but something just won't let me give up. I never took into account those Sundays when only eight people or nine people would show up or not having a drummer or a musician for months and having to lead praise and worship and I have little to no experience in this area. All I know is that I was called and I had been given a vision so I must go after it.

But now I'm standing in the midst of my process and its tougher than I imagined to keep going. For years, I didn't understand what it was that kept me going even though the results of the vision were not showing up. Then finally, one day, it hit me.

That thing called PASSION. Passion is something that is embedded deep down in a person and can only be measured by what they are willing to do and go through to accomplish the goal. This desire is there from the beginning. I believe you would not have had the dream without the desire to press through any obstacles that may come your way.

As much as you would like to give up its passion that speaks when the voices of failure have made there bold statements. Its passion that counter acts when every other solution is exhausted.

PASSION

Passion just won't let you throw in the towel when you have every reason to just give up because you realize the cost for what you are climbing towards is great!

Passion moves you to act when your situation is saying the contrary. Passion ignites in you when you have to burn the candle at both ends. Passion propels you past those that quit at any given moment because of their frustrations or reservations. This is something that you need to asses up front. Not only do you have what it takes but are you passionate about it?

Does this assignment on Earth illuminate from your very core to get it done no matter the cost? No matter the embarrassments? No matter the struggles? You may ask yourself, "Do I have what it takes? Well if you're passionate you will hang in there until you develop the skills necessary to be successful.

Passion gives you the innate ability to endure the development process of becoming more than you are at that very moment. You can see the gap in who you are and who you want to become. Let passion bridge the gap and drive you to your next destination.

Passion causes tears to run down your cheeks when you know you are hurting and it's hard to see your way but passion is there to hold you together when you are in a dozen pieces. Passion says lace up your boots, tighten the belt around your waist, straighten that crooked tie and hold your head because change is near.

Passion is the GPS of your purpose. It will direct you when you are lost and misguided because sometimes all you know is that you can't give up. So I challenge you as you reach new heights and places of elevation in your life to be passionate about your pursuit because you will find it can be a life saver. You can have passion for many different things. For instance, your calling, significant other, sports or family. When you are a person that is passionate about more than one area you have to be great at setting priorities for your life because if you don't you can have too many irons in the fire and not give enough to the most important at that time.

I had been on such a passionate journey to fulfill the call on my life before I started that all I did was write, pray, prepare sermons, listen to sermons meditate and attend church service and because of this my whole life suffered. For a season my kids got very little time and my wife also because I was so driven to change and become more. I was working on becoming a better minister but not a better father or husband. Talk about a miscalculation in priorities.

If I work on being a better father and husband I would naturally contribute to my development as a minister because after all my home was my ministry and if I failed at home I was failing altogether. So I had to reset my priorities and focus on my family and things going on in the home instead of burying myself in my ministry and neglected my top priorities. In changing my focus my home life became healthier.

Everyone was happier and I began to grow leaps and bounds because a lot of what I learned in the home contributed to my growth as a minster. All because I reset my priorities accurately I was able re–align my life with purpose and prepare myself for that point of elevation.

Chapter 10

AT THE POINT OF ELEVATION

As I contemplated what I would share in this chapter it became very clear to me. Most of the time when you use the word *elevation* automatically people think that you are talking about elevation from a financial or social point of view. Going higher on the totem pole or being promoted to a six-figure salary or being recognized globally for a specific gift or talent.

Now don't get me wrong, we all want to go higher in these arenas and truly you can elevate in these areas but when I talk of elevation I'm speaking from a spiritual standpoint. We can not only think of elevation from an external positioning but we must understand our growth from an internal perspective.

Are you growing and elevating in the things that truly matter? Like character. The definition of character is the aggregate of features and traits that form the individual nature of some

AT THE POINT OF ELEVATION

person or thing--one such feature or trait; characteristic, moral or ethical quality: *a man of fine, honorable character;* qualities of honesty, courage, or the like; integrity; reputation.

    Going to another level includes shaping a character that can be admired and trusted. When considering elevation you should start, I believe, with who you truly are verses who you want to be.

    Are you tired of making the same old mistakes. Are you looking in the mirror and seeing someone that you don't like. Do you find yourself responding to situations immorally and unethically? These are definitely character issues.

    How does one elevate from a poor character? I'm glad you asked. First you must be honest with yourself about the things in your life that God says are character flaws. You must genuinely assess yourself without being biased. Don't take it easy on yourself. Be detailed in your assessment and write down everything that you see that is hindering you from spiritual elevation.

Damion Jones

Use the spaces provided below to list ten character flaws that you would like to correct.

1._____
2._____
3._____
4._____
5._____
6._____
7._____
8._____
9._____
10._____

The next step to consider is to ask someone you trust like a mentor, pastor, father or mother etc., to give you ten things that they see and have experienced being in a relationship with you that are character flaws and need immediate addressing in order for you to go to your next place spiritually before the natural.

After you have received this list, use the spaces provided below to document it so you will have a visual of yourself from the point of view of another.

AT THE POINT OF ELEVATION

1._____
2._____
3._____
4._____
5._____
6._____
7._____
8._____
9._____
10._____

After you have gathered this information in its entirety you should have clear direction on where and what to improve upon in the area of character. As you begin to work on these character traits don't forget to reference your list and document those that you have made clear and honest improvements on. This project must first be put to much prayer and meditation. Prepare yourself for change because change will always cost you something.

This will not be an easy work but if you commit to it you will see great results. At the end of this chapter I have provided a space for you to document five areas in your character that you have improved upon.

Another place of spiritual elevation should be prayer and meditation. How much time do you spend with the Lord, the One who shapes character? Many of us want to change but we don't want to spend time with the one who can change us.

Prayer is essential to hearing from God on areas that the Lord desires us to change in so we can be who he called us to be. Prayer gets us ready to face the challenges of spiritual elevation and overcoming obstacles that may come our way. Prayer gives God opportunity to deposit new revelation, strength and power to you go to your next dimension. Every area of improvement or change should start with prayer.

In prayer God focuses us on what's important for the day or a specific season. It keeps us from being all over the place and taking on too much and frustrating ourselves. Prayer aligns us with daily elevation and positioning. God is the key to all elevation. In **Psalm 75:6-7,** its God who promotes and demotes (my paraphrase). So for any type of elevation especially spiritually we must go to the One who is in control. Another area of development in your spiritual life is meditation. The definition of

AT THE POINT OF ELEVATION

meditation is: the act of meditating.2. continued or extended thought; reflection; contemplation. 3. transcendental meditation. 4. devout religious contemplation or s spiritual introspection.

In order for you to grow you must visualize where you want to be. There must be a mental picture of your elevated place. How do you want to see yourself and what does that look like? You must put thought into the person that you want to be and take yourself mentally to that place so that you will know when you get there.

Meditate on your responses, tones ,interjections and demeanor. There must be time when you peacefully think things through to ensure the desired result. Sometime I close my self in my office turn off the lights and sit in the silence and I visualize where I'm at and where I want to be.

Then I focus on the steps that I need to take to get to my next place of elevation. I focus on the details in my journey and normally during this time I recognized something that I would have missed in my busy day. Meditation slows things down and allows you to carefully view the facts and see what you couldn't see in the normal pace of the day. There are times I recognize mistakes I've made and I'm able to make a mental correction or go back and make it right before it gets out of hand or yields a negative result. Meditation is crucial to your decision making and to your outlook on key situations in your life.

When you take time out to think things through and dream of a better future, you position yourself for a better outcome. You must realize that anything you focus on and take the proper steps towards will become a reality so take time to think it through. Take time to meditate and pull your thoughts together and shape a positive mental picture for your life.

God told Joshua in **Joshua 1:8,** "*This book of the law shall not depart out of thy mouth; but thou shalt MEDITATE therein day and night, that thou mayest observe to do according to all that is written therein: for then thou shalt make thy way prosperous, and then thou shalt have good success.*" (Emphasis mine. In order for Joshua to have success in his journey he was instructed to meditate on the book of the law and then success would be guaranteed. Meditation is key to you obtaining success in the arena that God is elevating you to. What you have on your mind continually you will eventually walk into. Meditation keeps you locked in and lined up with what you are pursuing. It keeps you in tune with your endeavor and puts you in pace with the heartbeat of the situation.

In **1 Timothy 4:15 It states to** - Meditate upon these things; give thyself wholly to them; that thy profiting may appear to all. Your meditation moments will shape your purpose into the reality you have dreamed of and become visible to those it is to benefit and be a message to.

Put your mind consistently and considerably on the things that you are going after and this act or action will cause you to live your dream before you actually live it. Spiritual elevation is the key to igniting your elevation and undeniable success in every other area of your life whether it be socially or financially.

We all want to go from one place to the other and we all want to live elevated in one way or another. For me I focused on what really matters and that's my spiritual growth in God which has brought about elevation in many areas of my life. My prayer is that you would use these principles shared in this book and achieve maximum success in each and every area of your life and that it would cause you to reach…your Point of Elevation in an healthy and honest way!

Use the space below to list at least 5 areas of your life that you have improved upon:

1. _____
2. _____
3. _____
4. _____
5. _____